Craving-worthy Cabbage Recipes: Irresistible Delights

Anand .R Serrano

*Craving-worthy Cabbage Recipes: Irresistible Delights :
Satisfy your Taste Buds with Easy-to-Make Cabbage Dishes.*

Funny helpful tips:

Avoid jumping to conclusions; seek clarity first.

Stay informed about your body's nutritional needs; as you age or change your training, these needs can shift.

Life advices:

Stay vigilant about the ethical implications of AI; its impact on jobs and decision-making requires thoughtful consideration.

In the meadow of dreams, chase your aspirations with unwavering belief.

Introduction

This book is a comprehensive guide that transforms the humble cabbage into a plethora of dishes that tantalize the taste buds and add a healthy twist to meals. With recipes ranging from appetizers and sides to hearty main dishes, this cookbook showcases the versatility of cabbage in various cuisines and cooking methods.

Start your culinary adventure with innovative appetizers like Cabbage Fritters and Cabbage Puff Pastries Triangles, perfect for kicking off any meal with a bang. For a unique twist, the Corned Beef Cabbage Dip or Crispy Cabbage Pancakes with Homemade Dipping Sauce offer flavorsome options for dipping and sharing.

Dive into the mains with dishes that highlight cabbage's ability to pair beautifully with a wide range of ingredients. The Baja Shrimp Taco Salad brings a fresh, seafood twist to the table, while the Beef and Rice Stuffed Whole Cabbage offers a hearty, comforting option. Vegetarians and vegans are not forgotten, with options like the Smoky Tofu and Cabbage Noodles and Veggie Curry providing delicious plant-based alternatives.

The cookbook also dedicates a special section to sides, where cabbage shines as a star ingredient. From Braised Red Cabbage with Spices and Apple to the innovative Cabbage Chips and Irish Colcannon, these recipes offer perfect accompaniments to any main dish or can be enjoyed on their own for a lighter meal.

Whether you're a cabbage enthusiast or simply looking to incorporate more vegetables into your diet, this book provides a treasure trove of recipes that will inspire you to view cabbage in a whole new light.

With dishes that range from simple to sophisticated, this cookbook ensures that there's something for every palate and occasion. Rediscover cabbage with these creative and delicious recipes, and make it a staple in your culinary adventures.

Contents

Appetizers and Sides

Cabbage Fritters

Enjoy these gorgeous cabbage fritters to serve with your favorite dip

Servings: 4

Total Prep Time: 10mins

Ingredients:

- 3 cups cooked cabbage (chopped)
- 2 medium size eggs
- ¼ cup panko breadcrumbs
- 2 tbsp fresh chives (chopped)
- 2 tbsp fresh parsley (chopped)
- Salt
- ¼ tsp coarsely ground black pepper

- ⅓ cup vegetable oil

Directions:

1. Add the chopped cabbage to a large bowl.

2. Stir in the eggs followed by the panko breadcrumbs, chives, and parsley. Season with salt and black pepper and mix to combine entirely.

3. Evenly divide the mixture into 8 portions and using clean hands form each portion into a patty.

4. Over moderate heat, in a skillet, heat the oil.

5. Add the cabbage fritters to the oil, slightly flatter and fry for 1-2 minutes on each side until gently browned and sufficiently cooked through.

6. Transfer to a kitchen paper towel-lined plate and season with additional salt.

7. Serve and enjoy.

vvvvvvvvvvvvvvvvvvvvvvvvvvvvvvvvvvvvvvvvvvvvvvvvvvvvv

Cabbage Puff Pastries Triangles

Pop in the mouth golden pastry parcels filled with shredded cabbage will have everyone coming back for more.

Servings: 18

Total Prep Time: 40mins

Ingredients:

- 1 (7¼ ounce) package frozen puff pastry sheets
- 3-4 tbsp vegetable oil
- 1 large onion (peeled, chopped)

- ½ medium-size cabbage (shredded)
- Salt and black pepper
- ½ tsp dried dill
- 1 egg (lightly beaten)

Directions:

1. Preheat the main oven to 400 degrees F.

2. Defrost the puff pastry at room temperature for a maximum of than 40 minutes.

3. In a pan heat the oil and add the chopped onion, cooking until translucent.

4. Next, add the shredded cabbage and cook until softened.

5. Taste and season with salt and pepper.

6. Stir in the dill and set to one side to cool for 2-3 minutes.

7. Roll the puff pastry sheet out and cut it into squares of your preferred size.

8. Add a spoonful of cabbage to the middle of each square, fold and with the help of a fork seal the edges and form a triangular shape.

9. Lightly brush the pastries with the beaten egg and arrange them on a parchment paper lined baking pan.

10. Bake the pastries in the preheated oven for between 15-17 minutes or until golden brown.

11. Serve and enjoy.

vvvvvvvvvvvvvvvvvvvvvvvvvvvvvvvvvvvvvvvvvvvvvvvvvvvvvvv

Corned Beef Cabbage Dip

Every bit as tasty as its main course counterpart, this delicious creamy dip makes an appetizing lite bite or snack.

Servings: 8

Total Prep Time: 30mins

Ingredients:

- 1 head green cabbage
- 2 (3 ounce) packages cream cheese (softened)
- ½ cup mayonnaise
- ¼ cup sour cream
- 2 tsp Worcestershire sauce
- 1 tsp fennel seeds
- Salt and black pepper
- 2 cups cooked corned beef (chopped)
- 1 cup Havarti cheese (shredded)

- ¼ cup Parmesan cheese (freshly grated)
- Crackers (to serve, optional)

Directions:

1. Hollow out the middle of the cabbage and chop the removed sections of cabbage and measure out 1 cup. Set the remaining cabbage aside for an alternate use.

2. In a bowl, beat the cream cheese until silky smooth.

3. Add the mayo and again beat to combine and until smooth.

4. Stir in the sour cream followed by the Worcestershire sauce, and fennel seeds. Season well with salt and black pepper.

5. Add the chopped cabbage along with the corned beef.

6. Fold in the shredded Havarti cheese.

7. Spoon the mixture into the hollowed out cabbage shell and transfer to the fridge until you are ready to serve.

8. Garnish with the freshly grated Parmesan cheese. Serve with crackers.

vvvvvvvvvvvvvvvvvvvvvvvvvvvvvvvvvvvvvvvvvvvvvvvvvvvv

Crispy Cabbage Pancakes with Homemade Dipping Sauce

Your veggie friends and family will love these crispy, golden cabbage pancakes.

Servings: 4

Total Prep Time: 25mins

Ingredients:

Dipping Sauce:

- 4 tbsp Greek yogurt
- 1 tbsp low-sodium soy sauce
- 1 tsp hot sauce

Pancakes:

- 8 ounces store-bought, shredded coleslaw mixture
- ½ cup scallions (sliced)
- 2 tbsp coconut flour
- 4 large eggs
- 1 tbsp low-sodium soy sauce
- ¼ tsp black pepper
- 1 tbsp garlic (peeled, minced)
- 1 tbsp coconut oil (to fry)

Directions:

1. In a small bowl, combine the dipping sauce ingredients in a bowl (Greek yogurt, soy sauce, and hot sauce). Set to one side.

2. In a mixing bowl, combine the coleslaw mixture with the scallions and coconut flour.

3. In a bowl, whisk the egg together with the soy sauce, black pepper, and garlic.

4. Stir the egg mixture into the cabbage mixture, mixing well to combine.

5. Over moderate to high heat, heat a griddle for a few minutes. Add 1 tablespoon of oil to the pan and brush to coat.

6. Scoop the mixture into the griddle using a 4 tbsp ice cream scoop. Flatten the mixture using a spatula.

7. Cook the pancakes for between 3-4 minutes on each side, until evenly browned. F

8. Serve with the dipping sauce and enjoy.

vvvvvvvvvvvvvvvvvvvvvvvvvvvvvvvvvvvvvvvvvvvvvvvvvvvvvv

Duck Tacos with Tomato-Cilantro Sauce

Tasty taco shells filled with juicy duck and a homemade creamy tomato-cilantro sauce.

Servings: 2-4

Total Prep Time: 2days 15mins

Ingredients:

Cilantro Sauce:

- 2 tbsp store-bought Ranch dressing

- 2 tbsp salsa fresco

Duck Tacos:

- 6 ounces duck breast (skinned, fat removed, cut into 3" strips)
- 1 tbsp olive oil
- 1 tbsp soy sauce
- 1 tbsp freshly squeezed lime juice
- ¼ cup sour cream
- 6 (3") taco shells
- Red and green cabbage (shredded)
- ¼ cup ripe tomatoes (diced)
- ¼ cup Greek feta cheese (crumbled)
- Cilantro leaves (chopped, to garnish)

Directions:

1. First, prepare the sauce: In a bowl combine the Ranch dressing and salsa fresco in a mixing well to fully incorporate.

2. Add the strips of duck along with the olive oil, soy sauce, and lime juice and marinate for between 12-24 hours.

3. Remove the duck from the marinade, and shake off any excess marinade.

4. Over high heat, in a saucepan, sauté the marinated duck strips until gently browned.

5. Place a small scoop of sour cream in the center of a plate.

6. Place the ends of the taco shells, standing upright, in the sour cream to create a fan shape around the plate.

7. Spoon the tomato-cilantro sauce into each one of the taco shells. Fill the shells with the duck.

8. Top each taco shell with cabbage followed by diced tomato, crumbled Feta cheese, and cilantro.

9. Enjoy.

vvvvvvvvvvvvvvvvvvvvvvvvvvvvvvvvvvvvvvvvvvvvvvvvvvvvvvvvvvvv

Grilled Caesar Cabbage

Fresh cabbage, golden raisins, and salty anchovy fillets come together to create an incredible warm Caesar cabbage appetizer.

Servings: 4

Total Prep Time: 45mins

Ingredients:

- 1 head green cabbage (quartered)
- Kosher salt and freshly ground black pepper
- ¼ cup olive oil
- 1 tbsp golden raisins (minced)

- 2 tbsp freshly squeezed orange juice
- 2 tsp capers (minced)
- 2 tsp anchovy fillets (minced) fillet for garnish
- 1 tsp orange zest
- 1 tsp fresh garlic (peeled, minced)
- 1 tsp chili paste
- 1 anchovy fillet (to garnish)
- 2 tbsp Grana Padano cheese (freshly grated)
- 2 tbsp toasted breadcrumbs (to garnish)

Directions:

1. Light the grill.

2. Season the cabbage with kosher salt and black pepper.

3. Place the cabbage quarters on the grill and cook, flipping over once, 7 minutes per side until well charred. Transfer the cabbage to a mixing bowl and cover with plastic kitchen wrap. Allow to steam until fork tender; this will take around 15 minutes.

4. In the meantime, in a smaller bowl, whisk the olive oil together with the raisins, fresh orange juice capers,, minced anchovies, orange zest, garlic, and chili paste. Season to taste with salt.

5. Remove the cabbage's core and slice the cabbage into 1" pieces,

6. Toss the cabbage with the dressing.

7. Transfer the cabbage to a plate and garnish with the remaining anchovy fillet, grated Grana Padano cheese and 2 tbsp of breadcrumbs

8. Serve and enjoy.

vvvvvvvvvvvvvvvvvvvvvvvvvvvvvvvvvvvvvvvvvvvvvvvvvvvvvvv

Instant Pot Borscht

Cook this Eastern European sour soup in a pressure cooker and serve with a large swirl of sour cream.

Servings: 8

Total Prep Time: 45mins

Ingredients:

- 1 tablespoon olive oil
- ½ pound carrots (shredded)
- ¼ pound onion (peeled, diced)
- 1 pound beets (diced into ¼" pieces)
- 1¾ pounds potatoes (peeled, cut into 1½" pieces)
- 1 pound cabbage (cored, shredded)
- 2 tbsp tomato paste
- 6 cups vegetable stock (warm)
- Dill (chopped)

- Salt and black pepper
- Sour cream (to serve)

Directions:

1. Switch your instant pot on and select the sauté option.

2. Add the olive oil to the pot, and heat until hot.

3. Add the remaining ingredients (carrots, onion, beets, potatoes, cabbage, tomato paste, and vegetable stock) to the pot and stir to combine.

4. Close the pot's lid, turn the valve to sealing, and select a cooking time of 13 minutes.

5. It will take between 15-30 minutes for the pot to come to pressure.

6. As soon as the 13 minutes of pressure cooking is up, and the cooker beeps release the pressure, and with a kitchen table carefully open the lid.

7. Garnish with chopped dill.

8. Season to taste with salt and pepper and serve with a swirl of sour cream.

vvvvvvvvvvvvvvvvvvvvvvvvvvvvvvvvvvvvvvvvvvvvvvvvvvvvvvvvv

Slow Cooker Cabbage Soup

This recipe requires lots of chopping but very little cooking. Pop it in your slow cooker and hey presto five hours later you have a warming, satisfying veggie soup to enjoy.

Servings: 12-14

Total Prep Time: 5hours 25mins

Ingredients:

- 1 small onion (peeled, diced)
- 2 cloves garlic (peeled, minced)
- 1 cup carrots (diced)

- 4 cups cabbage (chopped)
- 2 celery stalks (chopped)
- 1 cup green beans (chopped into 1" pieces)
- 2 whole bell peppers (chopped)
- 1 (28 ounce) can low sodium chopped or diced tomatoes
- 2 tbsp tomato paste
- 6 cups low sodium chicken broth
- 1½ tsp store-bought Italian seasoning
- 2 bay leaves
- Black pepper
- 1 tbsp parsley (chopped)
- 1 tbsp basil
- 2 cups fresh spinach (coarsely chopped)

Directions:

1. Combine the onion, garlic, carrots, cabbage, celery, green beans, bell peppers, and diced tomatoes in a slow cooker.

2. Add the tomatoes followed by the tomato paste, chicken broth, Italian seasoning, bay leaves, black pepper and stir thoroughly to combine entirely.

3. Cover, and on high cook for 5 hours or on low for 8 hours.

4. Once sufficiently cooked, add the chopped parsley along with the basil and spinach and cook for an additional 5 minutes.

5. Serve and enjoy.

Spicy Scallops on a Bed of Red Cabbage Citrus Slaw

Don't be put off preparing scallops at home, they are ready in minutes, and will bring sophistication to a number of dishes.

Servings: 2

Total Prep Time: 20mins

Ingredients:

Citrus Slaw:

- ½ cup freshly squeezed orange juice
- ¼ cup freshly squeezed lime juice
- ½ small red onion (peeled, coarsely chopped)
- 2 garlic cloves (peeled, minced)
- 2 tbsp fresh cilantro
- 1 tbsp honey
- ¼ cup canola oil
- ½ head red cabbage (shredded)

- Salt and black pepper

Scallops:

- 1 tsp cayenne pepper
- ½ tsp black pepper
- ½ tsp garlic powder
- 3 tbsp grapeseed oil
- ½ pound large scallops

Directions:

1. First, prepare the vinaigrette for the slaw: In a food blender, combine the fresh orange and lime juices along with the onion, garlic, cilantro, honey, and canola oil. Process until silky smooth.

2. Pour the vinaigrette over the shredded cabbage and season, tossing to evenly and well coat. Transfer to the fridge for 30-60 minutes, to marinate. Remember to toss every 15 minutes.

3. For the scallops: In a bowl, whisk the cayenne with the pepper, garlic powder and grapeseed oil. Pat the scallops dry using kitchen paper towel, toss in the scallops and evenly coat.

4. Over high heat, heat a large frying pan or skillet.

5. Add the scallops, leaving sufficient space between each scallop. Cook for 1 ½ -2 minutes on each side, flipping over once. There should be a ¼ "crust on each side.

6. Serve the scallops over the slaw.

Stuffed Pork and Cabbage Rolls

Rice, ground pork and cabbage rolls are the perfect weeknight appetizer or snack.

Servings: 8

Total Prep Time: 1hour 10mins

Ingredients:

- 10-12 cabbage Leaves (cored, brown leaves removed)
- ½ pound ground pork
- 1 tbsp garlic (peeled, minced)

- 1 tsp smoked paprika
- 2 tsp thyme
- ⅓ cup onions (peeled, finely chopped)
- 1 Large size egg
- 1 tsp salt
- 1½ tsp white pepper
- 2 tbsp parsley
- ½ tsp beef bouillon
- ⅓ cup cooked rice

Tomato Sauce:

- ¼ cup olive oil
- ½ cup onion (peeled, diced)
- 1 tsp thyme
- 2 tsp garlic (peeled, minced)
- ½-1 (14½ ounce) can tomato sauce
- 1 tsp Creole seasoning
- 1 tsp white pepper
- ½ tsp cayenne pepper
- 1 tsp smoked paprika
- ¼ cup chopped green pepper (chopped)
- 1-2 tsp beef bouillon
- 1 -2 cups chicken stock
- Salt (to season)

Directions:

1. Pour in sufficient water to fill a large pot.

2. Add the cabbage leaves to the pot and boil for approximately 4-5 minutes, until tender and pliable. Remove the pot from the stove top. Drain the hot water from the pot and add ice water. Set aside to cool.

3. Once the water is cool, remove the cabbage leaves. Using a paring knife, cut away the thick middle stem from each of the leaves while taking care not to cut all the way through; this will make folding a lot easier. Set to one side.

4. In a mixing bowl, combine the ground pork with the garlic, smoked paprika, thyme, onion, egg, salt, white pepper, parsley, beef bouillon and cooked rice. Mix thoroughly to incorporate.

5. Spoon between ¼-⅓ cup of the meat mixture into the middle of each cabbage leaf and tightly roll, tucking in the ends and securing with cocktail sticks.

6. Repeat the process until all the pork mixture is used. Put to one side.

7. For the tomato sauce: In a pan, add approximately a ¼ cup of oil and bring to moderate heat.

8. Add the onion along with the thyme and garlic to the oil, stirring for approximately 60 seconds.

9. Next, stir in the tomato sauce along with the Creole seasoning, white pepper, cayenne pepper, smoked paprika, and chopped green pepper. You will need to frequently stir to prevent the sauce from sticking to the pot.

10. Add the bouillon with 2 cups of stock. Bring to boil and allow to simmer for 15 minutes, while occasionally stirring — season with salt.

11. Transfer the sauce to a large casserole dish.

12. Place the cabbage rolls with the seam side facing down on top of the sauce. And bake in the oven until tender, for 45 minutes.

vvvvvvvvvvvvvvvvvvvvvvvvvvvvvvvvvvvvvvvvvvvvvvvvvvvvvvvvv

Thai Coconut Milk Soup

With so many ingredients, this soup recipe may seem complicated, but it is actually very simple to make, and well worth the effort!

Servings: 4

Total Prep Time: 30mins

Ingredients:

- 1 tbsp sesame oil (divided)
- 2-3 cups red or green cabbage (shredded)
- 1-2 tbsp freshly squeezed lime juice (divided)
- 1 tsp garlic (peeled, minced)
- Freshly ground black pepper
- 5 cups vegetable stock

- 2 stalks fresh lemongrass (cut into 1" pieces)
- ½ tsp ground curry
- 1 tsp ground ginger
- 1 tbsp red chili paste
- Splash of fish sauce
- 1¾ cups coconut milk
- 2 Thai bird's eyes red peppers (seeded, sliced, to garnish)
- Fresh cilantro (torn, to garnish)
- Slices of fresh lime

Directions:

1. Add the oil to a large pan and sauté the cabbage along with 1 tablespoon of fresh lime juice, garlic, and a dash of black pepper. Cook for approximately 2 minutes on moderate to moderate-high heat. It is important to only partially cook. Set to one side.

2. Using the same pan, add the stock, lemongrass, curry, ginger, chili paste. Allow to simmer for approximately 10 minutes, on moderate low while occasionally stirring.

3. When 10 minutes have elapsed, add the sautéed cabbage and a splash of fish sauce, ½ tablespoon of fresh lime juice and the coconut milk. Mix to combine and simmer for an additional 5-10 minutes.

4. Add the Thai bird's eye peppers and garnish with cilantro. Serve straight away with slices of lime.

vvvvvvvvvvvvvvvvvvvvvvvvvvvvvvvvvvvvvvvvvvvvvvvvvvv

Walnut and Cabbage Pate

Serve this veggie pate with toast, pita bread or veggie batons.

Servings: 12-15

Total Prep Time: 35mins

Ingredients:

- 3 pounds cabbage (cored, quartered)
- 1½ cups walnuts
- 1 cup onion (peeled, coarsely chopped)
- 2 teaspoons Asian chili paste
- 1 tsp salt
- 4 tbsp red wine vinegar

Directions:

1. Add the cabbage to a large pot and add sufficient water just to cover. Cover with a lid and bring to boil.

2. Cook the cabbage until fork tender, for 15-20 minutes. Drain and set aside to cool.

3. In a processor or food blender, finely mince the nuts. Set to one side.

4. Wash the processor/blender, and dry.

5. Add the onions to the clean processor blender and finely mince.

6. Press any excess water from the cabbage and add to the processor, processing until finely chopped.

7. Return the walnuts to the process, and add the chili paste, salt, and red wine vinegar, and process to entirely combine and transfer to the fridge to chill.

8. Serve with pita bread or veggie batons.

vvvvvvvvvvvvvvvvvvvvvvvvvvvvvvvvvvvvvvvvvvvvvvvvvvvv

Mains

vvvvvvvvvvvvvvvvvvvvvvvvvvvvvvvvvvvvvvvvvvvvvvvvvvvvvvvvvvvvv

Baja Shrimp Taco Salad

This main dish shrimp taco salad is a must for seafood lovers, and what's more, it's easy and quick to prepare.

Servings: 4

Total Prep Time: 40mins

Ingredients:

Dressing:

- ¾ cup sour cream
- Freshly squeezed juice of 2 medium limes
- ¼ cup loosely packed fresh cilantro (finely chopped)
- 2 tbsp water
- ½ tsp ground cumin

- ½ tsp kosher salt
- ⅛ tsp cayenne pepper

Salad:

- Nonstick cooking spray
- 1-pound uncooked medium shrimp (peeled, deveined)
- 1¼ tsp ground cumin
- ¾ tsp chili powder
- ½ tsp paprika
- ½ tsp kosher salt
- Freshly ground black pepper
- 1 tbsp freshly squeezed lime juice
- ½ large head red cabbage (thinly sliced)
- ⅓ cup fresh cilantro (finely chopped)
- 2 medium avocados (peeled, pitted, diced)
- 1 cup tortilla chips (crumbled)

Directions:

1. For the dressing: In a bowl, whisk the sour cream with the fresh lime juice, cilantro, water, ground cumin, kosher salt, and cayenne pepper. The mixture needs to be well combined and emulsified. Set to one side.

2. For the salad: Place a rack in the center of the oven and preheat to 400 degrees F. spray a rimmed baking tray with nonstick cooking spray and put to one side.

3. Using kitchen paper towel, pat the shrimp dry and arrange in an even layer on the baking tray.

4. Sprinkle cumin, chili powder, paprika, salt and 2-3 grinds of black pepper over the shrimp and stir to coat evenly.

5. Roast until the shrimp are pink and opaque for between 6-8 minutes in total.

6. Drizzle the lime juice over the cooked shrimp and toss to combine evenly. Set to one side.

7. Add the cabbage, cilantro and approximately half of the dressing in a large salad bowl and toss to combine entirely.

8. Top the salad with the shrimp and avocado and drizzle with the remaining dressing.

9. Garnish with crumbled chips and serve.

vvvvvvvvvvvvvvvvvvvvvvvvvvvvvvvvvvvvvvvvvvvvvvvvvvvvvv

Baked Cajun Cabbage Casserole

A Cajun-spiced casserole will tick all the taste boxes and satisfy even the hungriest of tummies.

Servings: 6

Total Prep Time: 1hour 5mins

Ingredients:

- 1 large head cabbage (outer leaves removed, cored chopped into bite-size pieces)
- 1 cup onion (peeled, chopped)
- 1 cup celery (chopped)
- 1 cup bell pepper (chopped)
- Salt
- Pinch of cayenne pepper

Cheese Sauce:

- ½ cup butter
- 4 tbsp flour
- 1½ cups milk
- ½ pound mature Cheddar cheese (grated)

Topping:

- 1 cup green onions (chopped)
- ¼ cup seasoned breadcrumbs

Directions:

1. In a pot of water, boil the cabbage, uncovered for 10 minutes, until tender crisp. Drain and put to one side.

2. For the sauce: In a separate pan, combine the butter with the flour over medium heat, stirring to blend.

3. Add the onions along with the celery, bell pepper, salt, and cayenne and sauté for 10 minutes.

4. Pour in the milk and over low heat, stir until creamy and well combined.

5. Fold in the Cheddar cheese until blended and smooth.

6. Transfer the cabbage into a casserole dish, of 2-quart capacity, and top with the cheesy sauce.

7. Scatter the seasoned breadcrumbs over the top.

8. Bake in the oven at 350 degrees F for half an hour until bubbling and sufficiently heated through.

vvvvvvvvvvvvvvvvvvvvvvvvvvvvvvvvvvvvvvvvvvvvvvvvvvvvvvvvv

Beef and Rice Stuffed Whole Cabbage

An impressive meal to wow your family and friends, this main is sure to impress.

Servings: 8

Total Prep Time: 1hour

Ingredients:

Sauce:

- 1 (28 ounce) can diced tomatoes (undrained)
- 1 (6 ounce) can tomato paste
- 1 clove garlic (peeled, minced)
- 1½ tsp dried oregano

- 1 tsp dried thyme
- 1 tsp brown sugar
- ½ tsp salt

Filling:

- 1-pound ground beef
- 1 medium-size onion (peeled, chopped)
- 1 large head cabbage
- ¾ cup cooked rice
- 1 medium-size egg (beaten)
- 1 tsp salt
- ½ tsp pepper
- 2¼ cups water (divided)
- 3 tbsp cornstarch
- 2 tbsp Parmesan cheese (shredded)

Directions:

1. Combine the tomatoes with the tomato paste, garlic, oregano, thyme, brown sugar, and salt. Set to one side.

2. In a frying pan, cook the beef along with the onion, until the meat is gently browned and the onion tender. Remove from the heat and drain off the oil.

3. Prepare the cabbage: Leave a 1" shell and the core intact, cut out and with a sharp knife cut the inside of the cabbage.

4. Add 1 cup of chopped cabbage to the beef followed by 1 cup of sauce, rice, egg, salt, and black pepper, and mix thoroughly to combine.

5. Spoon the beef mixture into the cabbage shell.

6. Pour 2 cups of water and the remaining cabbage, and remaining sauce into a Dutch oven, and stir to combine.

7. Carefully add the stuffed cabbage to the Dutch oven, meat side facing upwards.

8. Cover and bring to boil before reducing the heat, covering and simmer for 90 minutes, until the whole cabbage is tender.

9. Remove the cabbage from the Dutch oven and transfer to a serving plate and keep warm.

10. In a small bowl, combine the cornstarch with the remaining water, and add to the Dutch oven.

11. Bring to boil, while continually stirring, for a couple of minutes.

12. Pour the mixture over the cabbage.

13. Scatter the parmesan over the top, cut into wedges and enjoy.

vvvvvvvvvvvvvvvvvvvvvvvvvvvvvvvvvvvvvvvvvvvvvvvvvvvvvvvvvv

Beef Lasagna with Cabbage

Add protein to this classic pasta dish by adding green cabbage to your favorite lasagna dish.

Servings: 8

Total Prep Time: 1hour 10mins

Ingredients:

- 2 tbsp extra virgin olive oil
- 1 onion (peeled, chopped)
- 2 garlic cloves (peeled, minced)
- 1½ pounds ground beef
- 2 (14 ounce) cans crushed tomatoes

- 1 tbsp balsamic vinegar
- Salt and black pepper
- ¼ cup basil leaves (torn)
- 3 cups ricotta
- 2 medium-eggs (beaten)
- ¼ cup Parmesan (freshly grated)
- 3 cups mozzarella (shredded)
- 1 large head cabbage leaves (separated)

Directions:

1. Preheat the main oven to 350 degrees F.

2. Over moderate heat, in a frying pan, heat the oil.

3. Add the onion and cook for 5 minutes, until softened.

4. Stir in the garlic along with the ground beef and using the back of a wooden spoon, break up the meat.

5. Continue to cook the meat until no pink remains, approximately 5-6 minutes. Drain the excess fat.

6. Add the crushed tomatoes along with the vinegar.

7. Bring the mixture to boil before reducing to simmer for 20 minutes. Season with the black pepper and kosher salt and fold in the basil.

8. In a bowl, combine the ricotta with the eggs and freshly grated Parmesan.

9. Grease lightly a casserole dish with the olive oil.

10. Spoon a thin layer of sauce into the casserole dish.

11. Add a layer of cabbage leaves and then top with additional sauce, the ricotta mixture and mozzarella cheese.

12. Repeat the process, layering another two times.

13. Bake in the oven until the cabbage is tender and the mozzarella cheese is bubbling, this will take approximately 25 minutes.

14. Serve and enjoy.

vvvvvvvvvvvvvvvvvvvvvvvvvvvvvvvvvvvvvvvvvvvvvvvvvvvvvvvvv

Burrito-Stuffed Cabbage Rolls

This lightened up version of your favorite Mexican dish swaps carby tortillas for low-calorie cabbage wraps.

Servings: 4

Total Prep Time: 1hour 10mins

Ingredients:

- 2 cups tomato salsa
- 1 head Savoy cabbage
- 1 tbsp kosher salt
- 1-pound lean ground beef
- 1 (1 ounce) sachet taco seasoning
- 1 tomato (seeded, chopped)

- 1 cup cooked long-grain white rice
- 2 cups Mexican blend cheese (shredded, divided)

To Serve:

- Pickled jalapeno slices
- Sliced scallions
- Sour cream

Directions:

1. Arrange a rack in the center of the oven and heat to 375 degrees F. Pour 1½ cups of the tomato salsa in an even layer into a 9x13" casserole dish and set to one side.

2. Bring a large pan of water to boil.

3. In the meantime, remove between 10-12 whole outer leaves from the cabbage.

4. Stir the kosher salt into the boiling water and add the cabbage leaves, cooking until they begin to wilt, for approximately 2 minutes. Remove the cabbage leaves with kitchen tongs and transfer to a kitchen paper towel-lined baking sheet and set aside to cool.

5. Place the ground beef in a large mixing bowl, sprinkle with the taco seasoning, and using clean hands gently mix to combine without compacting the meat. Evenly divide the mixture into 8 portions and form each portion into a slider-sized patty; set to one side.

6. Divide the tomatoes, white rice, and 1 cup of the Mexican blend cheese evenly among the largest 8 cabbage leaves.

7. Top each one with a beef patty. Working with one cabbage leaf at a time, fold the right and left sides of the leaf over the filling. From the bottom, up tightly roll to form a cabbage roll.

8. Place seam-side facing down in the salsa in the casserole dish. Repeat the process making the remaining cabbage rolls.

9. Spoon the remaining ½ cup of salsa over the cabbage rolls. Scatter with the remaining cheese.

10. Bake in the oven until the cheese begins to melt and brown, the cabbage is tender, and the filling registers 165 degrees F on an internal thermometer, about half an hour.

11. Top with jalapeños, scallions, and a dollop of sour cream.

vvvvvvvvvvvvvvvvvvvvvvvvvvvvvvvvvvvvvvvvvvvvvvvvvvv

Cabbage Dumplings in Curry Gravy

Cabbage dumplings with a spicy filling served with a curry flavor gravy will have everyone coming back for more.

Servings: 6

Total Prep Time: 45mins

Ingredients:

Cabbage Dumplings:

- 2 cups green cabbage (finely shredded)
- 1 tbsp coconut oil
- ¼ cup onion (peeled, finely chopped)
- 2 cloves garlic (peeled, minced)
- ¼ tsp coriander
- ¼ tsp cumin powder
- ¼ cup chickpea flour

- 2 tbsp water (as needed)
- ½ tsp kosher salt

Gravy:

- 1 tbsp coconut oil
- 1 small onion (peeled, finely chopped)
- 2 cloves garlic (peeled, minced)
- 1 tsp ginger (minced)
- 1 medium tomato (chopped)
- 2 tsp curry powder
- ½ tsp ground paprika
- 1 cup coconut milk
- 1 cup water
- 1 tsp salt
- ¼ tsp cayenne pepper
- ¼ cup cashews + ½ cup water
- 2 tbsp cilantro leaves (chopped, to garnish)

Directions:

1. Add the cabbage to a food processor. On the pulse setting, finely shred.

2. Transfer the shredded cabbage to a bowl and put to one side.

3. Preheat the main oven to 400 degrees F. Lightly grease a baking sheet and put to one side.

4. Over moderate heat, in a skillet, heat the oil.

5. Add the onion along with the garlic to the skillet and cook until the onion is softened.

6. Stir in the coriander followed by the cumin and cook for an additional 60 seconds.

7. Add the shredded cabbage and cook while stirring for 5 minutes until the cabbage is fork tender season to taste.

8. Transfer the cabbage to a mixing bowl and set aside to cool.

9. Stir in the chickpea flour and mix thoroughly to create a dough. You may need to add a drop of water to help bring the dough together.

10. Shape the dough into equal sized dumplings and arrange on a baking sheet. Bake in the oven for between 25-30 minutes, turning after 15 minutes.

11. In the meantime, prepare the gravy. In a large pan over moderate heat, heat the oil.

12. Add the onion and cook for 4 minutes, until softened.

13. Add the garlic followed by the ginger and cook for approximately 60 seconds.

14. Stir in the tomatoes and cook for an additional 2 minutes.

15. Add the curry powder followed by the paprika while continually stirring for 60 seconds.

16. Pour in the coconut milk together with the water and add salt and cayenne to taste. Cover the pan with a lid and bring to boil.

17. Reduce to a simmer and simmer for approximately 10 minutes.

18. In the meantime, blend the cashews with the water.

19. Add the cashew mixture to the curry gravy while stirring and cook until thickened.

20. Turn the heat off. Add the cabbage dumpling and stir.

21. Garnish with cilantro leaves and serve with potatoes or rice.

vvvvvvvvvvvvvvvvvvvvvvvvvvvvvvvvvvvvvvvvvvvvvvvvvv

Creamy Cabbage Gratin with Bacon and Mushrooms

With gruyere cheese, bacon, wild mushrooms, and crunchy walnuts this gratin is rich and indulgent. The perfect weekend treat to share with family and friends.

Servings: 8

Total Prep Time: 2hours 15mins

Ingredients:

- Nonstick cooking spray
- 6 ounces of bacon (cut crosswise into thin strips)
- 1 medium-size yellow onion (peeled, thinly sliced)
- 1 large cabbage (cored, coarsely chopped)

- ¼ cup all-purpose flour
- 8 ounces of fresh wild mushrooms (chopped)
- 2 cups whole milk (warm)
- 2 cups Gruyere cheese (grated, divided)
- 1 tsp kosher salt
- 1 tsp freshly ground black pepper
- 1 tsp dry mustard
- ½ tsp freshly grated nutmeg
- ½ tsp cayenne pepper
- ½ cup walnuts (chopped)
- Parsley leaves (chopped, to garnish)

Directions:

1. Place a rack in the middle of the oven and preheat to 350 degrees F.

2. Lightly coat a 9" square casserole dish with nonstick cooking spray. Set to one side.

3. Add the bacon to a Dutch oven over moderate heat until the bacon is crispy and the fat is rendered, while occasionally stirring for 15 minutes.

4. With a slotted spoon, transfer the bacon to a bowl.

5. Pour all but 1 tsp of the bacon fat into a small heatproof bowl. Put the bacon fat to one side.

6. Add the mushrooms to the pot and over moderate heat, cook while occasionally stirring for 4 minutes, until browned and tender. Transfer the mushrooms to the bowl containing the bacon.

7. Add 1 tbsp of the bacon fat to the pot.

8. Add the onions along with a large pinch of salt and cook while occasionally stirring for 3 minutes, until wilted. You may need to add

a splash of water to loosen any browned bits from the bottom of the pot.

9. In batches, add the cabbage, stirring after every batch until it begins to wilt and before you add the next batch.

10. Cook while occasionally stirring until the cabbage is crisp but tender, this will take around 10 minutes. You may need to add a splash of water to prevent sticking.

11. Remove from the heat and cover with a lid to keep warm.

12. In a pan, over moderate to high heat, heat 2 tbsp of the bacon fat.

13. Sprinkle in the flour and whisk well until silky smooth.

14. Cook to remove the taste of the raw flour and continue to slowly whisk for 2 minutes. The roux will thicken and bubble.

15. Whisk in the warm milk until silky smooth and cook while slowly stirring with a rubber spatula for 3 minutes, until the sauce thickens and bubbles.

16. Add 1½ cups of the Gruyere cheese along with 1 tsp of salt, mustard, pepper, cayenne and nutmeg.

17. Continue to stir until the cheese entirely melts.

18. Stir in the reserved bacon and mushrooms.

19. Transfer the mixture to the pot of cabbage, stirring until well coated.

20. Transfer the cabbage mixture to the prepared casserole dish.

21. Sprinkle the remaining Gruyere over the top and bake in the oven until golden and bubbling for approximately half an hour.

22. Set the casserole aside to cool before serving.

23. When you are ready to serve, garnish with the walnuts and parsley.

French-Style Cabbage and Beans with Hake

Getting its inspiration from a French peasant dish this one-pot meal is flavorful, filling and family-friendly.

Servings: 4

Total Prep Time: 50mins

Ingredients:

- Small knob of butter
- 5 slices smoked streaky bacon (chopped)
- 1 red onion (peeled, finely chopped)
- 2 sticks of celery (diced)
- 2 carrots (diced)
- Handful fresh thyme
- 1 Savoy cabbage (shredded)

- 4 tbsp white wine
- 1¼ cups chicken stock
- 1 (14½) ounce can flageolet beans in water (drained)
- Salt and black pepper

Fish:

- 4 (5 ounce) skin-on hake fillets
- 2 tbsp plain flour
- 2 tbsp olive oil

Directions:

1. In a large frying pan, heat the butter.

2. Once the butter begins to sizzle, add the bacon, and fry for 2-3 minutes.

3. Next, add the onion along with the celery and carrots and gently cook for between 8-10 minutes, until beginning to soften but not brown.

4. Stir in the thyme along with the cabbage and cook for 2-3 minutes, until the cabbage starts to wilt.

5. Pour in the white wine and simmer until evaporated before adding the chicken stock and flageolet beans. Season, and cover the pan.

6. Gently simmer for 10 minutes, until the cabbage is vibrant and soft.

7. Once the cabbage is sufficiently cooked, prepare the fish.

8. Season the hake and dust the skin with plain flour.

9. In a frying pan, heat the oil.

10. Add the fish, skin side facing down to the pan and fry for 4-5 minutes until crisp. Flip the hake over and fry on the fleshy side until sufficiently cooked through.

11. Serve the fish and enjoy.

vvvvvvvvvvvvvvvvvvvvvvvvvvvvvvvvvvvvvvvvvvvvvvvvvvvvvvvvvvvvvvvvvvv

One-Pot Cabbage and Sausage Noodle Pasta

What could be easier than this one-pot pasta? All the flavor, all the taste but with none of the washing-up or hassle.

Servings: 6-8

Total Prep Time: 55mins

Ingredients:

- 8 ounces dried wide egg noodles
- 1 cup frozen green peas
- 3 tbsp unsalted butter (divided)
- 12 ounces fully cooked smoked sausage (cut into ½" rounds)
- 1 large yellow onion (peeled, halved, finely sliced)

- 1 red bell pepper (cored, thinly sliced)
- Pinch of kosher salt
- 1 medium cabbage (cored, quartered, shredded)
- Freshly ground black pepper

Directions:

1. Over high heat, bring a deep pot of salty water to boil.

2. Add the noodles and then cook for 2-3 minutes less than directed on the package instructions.

3. Stir in the frozen peas and cook until al dente for an additional couple of minutes. Drain thoroughly.

4. Return the noodles along with the peas tot the warm pot and stir in 1 tbsp of butter. Remove the pan out of the heat and Cover with a lid to keep warm.

5. Over moderate heat, in another pot, melt 1 tbsp of butter.

6. Add the sausage to the melted butter and while occasionally stirring cook for 5 minutes, until browned.

7. Using a slotted spoon, move the sausage to a bowl and put to one side.

8. Add the remaining butter to the empty pot and melt.

9. Stir in the yellow onion along with the bell pepper and a generous pinch of salt.

10. Cook while occasionally stirring for 5 minutes, until the veggies are starting to soften.

11. In batches, add the cabbage, stirring in between batches until each batch is beginning to wilt.

12. Cover with a lid and cook while occasionally stirring until the veggies are crisp yet tender, for approximately 10 minutes.

13. Stir in the drained noodles along with the peas and sausage set aside earlier.

14. Taste, season, serve and enjoy.

vvvvvvvvvvvvvvvvvvvvvvvvvvvvvvvvvvvvvvvvvvvvvvvvvvvvvvvv

Pasta and Red Potatoes with Cabbage

Pasta and potatoes are a popular pairing in southern Italy, and this dish featuring green cabbage makes a marvelous, healthy main course that the whole family can enjoy.

Servings: 4

Total Prep Time: 25mins

Ingredients:

- ½ pound red potatoes
- 8 ounces dry, whole wheat pasta
- 2 tbsp extra-virgin olive oil
- 1 clove garlic (peeled, minced)

- 2 baby heads green cabbage (cored, shredded)
- Salt and freshly ground pepper
- 1 tbsp butter
- ½ cup Grana Padano cheese (grated)

Directions:

1. Add the potatoes to a large pot and pour in sufficient cool water to cover.

2. Add 1 teaspoon of salt and bring to a boil over moderate-high heat.

3. Turn the heat down to a simmer and cook until the potatoes are fork tender. Using a slotted spoon scoop out the potatoes while leaving the pot of water on the stovetop.

4. If necessary, add water to the pot, and return to a boil.

5. Stir in the pasta and cook until the pasta is al dente.

6. Scoop out approximately a ½ cup of the pasta cooking water and set to one side. Drain the pasta.

7. In the meantime, heat a large, pan, and add the olive oil along with the garlic and cook until the garlic starts to sizzle. Add the cabbage and season with a pinch of salt and pepper.

8. Cook, while occasionally stirring for 2-3 minutes, or until cabbage softens.

9. Transfer the potatoes followed by the pasta to the pan of cabbage together with the ½ cup of the pasta water.

10. Stir in the butter and grated cheese, tossing to combine thoroughly — taste and season with salt and pepper.

11. Toss again and serve.

Roast Brussels Sprouts and Red Cabbage Pizza

Forget your usual pizza toppings and instead opt for this healthy veggie version featuring roasted sprouts and red cabbage.

Servings: 4-6

Total Prep Time: 45mins

Ingredients:

Sprouts:

- ½ pound Brussels sprouts (trimmed, halved)
- 1 tbsp olive oil

- 1 garlic clove (peeled, minced)
- 1 tbsp runny honey
- ¼ tsp salt
- Pinch red pepper flakes

Pizza:

- 1-pound refrigerated pizza dough
- Cornmeal (for dusting)
- 1 tbsp olive oil
- 1¼ cups mozzarella cheese (shredded, divided)
- ¾ cup red cabbage (shredded)
- ¼ cup toasted walnuts (chopped)
- Zest of 1 lemon (to garnish)

Directions:

1. Preheat the main oven to 400 degrees F.

2. Place the sprouts on a rimmed baking sheet and drizzle with olive oil followed by the garlic, honey, salt, and red pepper flakes, and toss to combine.

3. Bake in the preheated oven for between 12-15 minutes, stirring halfway through cooking, and cook until fork tender. Set to one side to slightly cool.

4. For the pizza: Increase the temperature of the oven to 500 degrees F. Place a pizza stone in the oven to heat.

5. In the meantime, on a well floured, clean work surface, roll the pizza dough out.

6. Move the dough to a sheet of parchment paper that has been lightly dusted with cornmeal.

7. Brush the pizza dough with oil.

8. Top the dough with 1 cup of mozzarella cheese.

9. Next, add the shredded cabbage, walnuts, roasted sprouts, and the remaining mozzarella cheese.

10. Transfer the pizza while still on the parchment paper, directly onto the hot pizza stone and bake in the oven for 10-15 minutes, until the crust is golden and the cheese bubbling.

11. Garnish with lemon zest and slice.

vvvvvvvvvvvvvvvvvvvvvvvvvvvvvvvvvvvvvvvvvvvvvvvvvvvvvvvvv

Slow Cooker Creamy Cabbage and Pork Stew

Easy to make and super-satisfying, this cabbage and pork stew is a great meal to come home to!

Servings: 6

Total Prep Time: 6hours 15mins

Ingredients:

- 1 tbsp canola oil
- 1-pound pork stew meat

- 3 cups cabbage (coarsely chopped)
- 2 (10¾) cans condensed cream of celery soup (undiluted)
- 1½ cups apple juice
- 2 red potatoes (cut into 1" pieces)
- 3 carrots (sliced)
- ¼ tsp caraway seeds
- ¼ tsp pepper
- ½ cup 2% milk

Directions:

1. Over moderate to high heat, in a large frying pan heat the oil. Add the pork and brown all over. Drain.

2. Transfer the meat to a slow cooker of 3-quart capacity.

3. Stir in the cabbage followed by the condensed soup, apple juice, red potatoes, carrots, caraway, and black pepper.

4. Cover and cook on low for between 6-8 hours, until the veggies are fork tender, and the meat is cooked through.

5. Stir in the milk and heat through.

6. Serve and enjoy.

vvvvvvvvvvvvvvvvvvvvvvvvvvvvvvvvvvvvvvvvvvvvvvvvvvvvvv

Smoky Tofu and Cabbage Noodles

This flavorful pasta featuring smoky tofu and cabbage makes a filling main midweek meal.

Servings: 4

Total Prep Time: 40mins

Ingredients:

- 6 ounces dried mafalada or flat ribbon-like pasta

- 2 tbsp soy sauce
- 1 tbsp pure maple syrup
- 1 tsp liquid smoke
- 1 tsp apple cider vinegar
- ¼ cup butter (divided)
- 7 ounces extra firm tofu (drained, pressed)
- 1 large onion (peeled, diced)
- 5 cups cabbage (chopped)
- 2 garlic cloves (peeled, minced)
- 1 tsp caraway seeds
- ½ cup sauerkraut
- Fresh parsley (chopped, to serve)

Directions:

1. Bring a large pan of salted water to boil and add the pasta.

2. Cook the pasta until al dente, drain and set to one side.

3. In a small bowl, combine the soy sauce with the maple syrup, liquid smoke, and apple cider vinegar.

4. Coat a large frying pan with 1 tbsp of butter and place it over moderate heat.

5. In an even layer, add the tofu to the hot butter and cook for 10 minutes, while flipping over 1 or 2 times, until browned all over.

6. Pour the soy sauce mixture over the tofu and cook until the majority of the liquid has dried up, for an additional 1-2 minutes longer.

7. Remove the tofu from the pan and transfer to a serving plate.

8. Add the remaining butter to the pan, and heat.

9. Add the onion and cabbage to the melted butter and sauté for 10 minutes, until fork tender.

10. Add the garlic and cook for an additional 60 seconds, until fragrant.

11. Add the drained noodles followed by the tofu, caraway, and sauerkraut to the pan and cook for an additional 2-3 minutes, until heated through.

12. Dive the mixture onto plates and garnish with parsley.

13. Serve and enjoy.

vvvvvvvvvvvvvvvvvvvvvvvvvvvvvvvvvvvvvvvvvvvvvvvvvvvvvv

Veggie Curry

This veggie curry is made with green cabbage, creamy coconut milk and spices and is a healthy alternative to take-out.

Servings: 4

Total Prep Time: 30mins

Ingredients:

- 1-pound green cabbage (washed, dried, chopped into 1" thick strips)
- 2 tbsp coconut oil
- ½ cup onion (peeled, chopped)

- 2 cloves garlic (peeled, minced)
- 1 tsp ground coriander
- 1 tsp ground turmeric
- 1 tsp dried thyme leaves
- ½ tsp cumin
- 1 carrot (chopped)
- 1 (14 ounce) can coconut milk
- ½ cup water
- ¾ tsp sea salt

Directions:

1. Add the strips of cabbage to a bowl and set to one side.

2. Over moderate-high heat, heat the oil in a large pan.

3. Add the onion along with the garlic and cook while stirring until softened, for 3 minutes.

4. Add the coriander along with the turmeric, thyme, cumin, carrot, and cabbage and stir.

5. Pour in the coconut milk, water and bring to boil.

6. Cover the pan with a lid and reduce to a simmer.

7. Cook for approximately 20 minutes, until the sauce, begins to thicken. Season with salt.

8. Serve with brown rice.

vvvvvvvvvvvvvvvvvvvvvvvvvvvvvvvvvvvvvvvvvvvvvvvvvvvvv

Sides

vvvvvvvvvvvvvvvvvvvvvvvvvvvvvvvvvvvvvvvvvvvvvvvvvvvvvvvvvv

Braised Red Cabbage with Spices and Apple

Braising red cabbage with fragrant cinnamon and star anise and adding crunchy apple, creates an aromatic and delicious side dish which is ideal for elevating mild-tasting chicken and turkey!

Servings: 8

Total Prep Time: 50mins

Ingredients:

- 1 red cabbage (shredded finely)
- 5 star anise
- 2 bay leaves
- ¾ cup + 1 tbsp vegetable stock

- ½ tsp cinnamon
- ⅓ cup apple cider vinegar
- 4 tbsp brown sugar
- 2 apples (cored, sliced into wedges)

Directions:

1. To a large saucepan over moderate heat, add the cabbage, star anise, bay leaves, stock, cinnamon, vinegar, and brown sugar. Bring to a boil then reduce to a simmer and cook for half an hour.

2. Add the apple and cook for another 15 minutes.

3. Stir well and serve straight away.

vvvvvvvvvvvvvvvvvvvvvvvvvvvvvvvvvvvvvvvvvvvvvvvvvvvvvv

Cabbage Chips

Crispy, crunch cabbage chips are a healthy alternative to potato chips, but what is even better is they taste good too.

Servings: 2-4

Total Prep Time: 50mins

Ingredients:

- ½ small head of cabbage
- ½ tsp extra-virgin olive oil
- Sea salt

Directions:

1. Preheat the main oven to 300 degrees.

2. Tear off the cabbage leaves into large pieces and toss well in olive oil — season with sea salt.

3. Arrange the cabbage in a single layer on two wire baking racks, set on rimmed baking racks.

4. Bake the cabbage in the oven until the leaves are beginning to slightly darken and crisp. Remove the leaves as they brown. This will take between 25-35 minutes.

5. Set aside to completely cool and serve.

vvvvvvvvvvvvvvvvvvvvvvvvvvvvvvvvvvvvvvvvvvvvvvvvvvvvv

Cabbage Hash Browns

It really is possible to enjoy crispy potato-free hash browns, and they are delicious served with crisp bacon and a sunny-side-up egg.

Servings: 2

Total Prep Time: 15mins

Ingredients:

- 2 large eggs
- ½ tsp garlic powder
- ½ tsp kosher salt
- Dash of freshly ground black pepper
- 2 cups cabbage (shredded)
- ¼ small yellow onion (peeled, thinly sliced)
- 1 tbsp vegetable oil

Directions:

1. In a bowl, whisk the eggs with the garlic powder, salt and a dash of pepper.

2. Add the cabbage along with the onion to the egg mixture and toss to combine.

3. Over moderate-high heat and in a large frying pan, heat the oil.

4. Evenly divide the mixture into 4 patties.

5. Add the patties to the pan, gently press them with a spatula to flatten,

6. Cook the patties for 3 minutes on each side, until golden brown.

7. Serve and enjoy.

vvvvvvvvvvvvvvvvvvvvvvvvvvvvvvvvvvvvvvvvvvvvvvvvvvvvvvvv

Cheese and Chive Slaw

A creamy coleslaw is the perfect side dish. It pairs with all number of recipes, transforming a mundane meal or snack into a great one!

Servings: 4-6

Total Prep Time: 25mins

Ingredients:

- 14 ounces white cabbage (halved, quartered, cored, thinly shredded.
- 1 carrot (coarsely grated)
- 1 red onion (peeled, halved, thinly sliced)
- 3 tbsp premium-quality mayonnaise
- 3 tbsp low-fat plain yogurt
- 1 tsp Dijon mustard
- 1 (¾ ounce) pack of chives
- 3 ounces low-fat mature cheddar (grated)

Directions:

1. Add the shredded cabbage to a large bowl.

2. Add the carrots along with the onion, mayonnaise, yogurt, and Dijon mustard.

3. Snip in the majority of the chives.

4. Using clean hands fully combine the ingredients, making sure all the veggies are entirely coated in the creamy dressing.

5. Season to taste.

6. Cover and chill in the fridge.

7. Remove from the fridge, scatter with grated cheese and garnish with the remaining chives.

vvvvvvvvvvvvvvvvvvvvvvvvvvvvvvvvvvvvvvvvvvvvvvvvvvvvvv

Fried Cabbage with Bacon

You can't go wrong with this tasty side dish and what's more, it's good to go in just 15 minutes.

Servings: 4

Total Prep Time: 15mins

Ingredients:

- 8 rashers bacon (coarsely chopped)
- 1 white onion (peeled, finely diced)

- 1 head green cabbage (cored, cut into 1" pieces)
- 1 tsp sugar
- Salt and black pepper
- 1 tbsp parsley (chopped)

Directions:

1. In a pan over moderate heat, cook the bacon for 4-5 minutes, until browned.

2. Add the onion and cook until translucent, for 3-4 minutes.

3. Put the cabbage into the pan along with the sugar, salt, and black pepper.

4. Cook, while occasionally stirring until the cabbage wilts. You might need to add a drop of water at this stage.

5. Garnish with parsley and serve.

vvvvvvvvvvvvvvvvvvvvvvvvvvvvvvvvvvvvvvvvvvvvvvvvvvvvvvvv

Green Cabbage with Creamy Juniper Sauce

Did you know that juniper berries and gin are the perfect ingredients to serve with cabbage? The fromage frais compliments the juices, creating a thin consistency sauce which is delicious over rice, noodles or pork.

Servings: 8

Total Prep Time: 45mins

Ingredients:

- 2 tsp juniper berries

- 3 tbsp gin
- 3½ ounces whole milk
- 1 large green cabbage
- 1 large leek (trimmed)
- ⅓ cup unsalted butter
- 1 tsp vegetable bouillon powder
- Salt and black pepper
- 8 ounces full-fat fromage fraise

Directions:

1. Add the berries to a ziplock bag and with a rolling pin, crush.

2. Add the crushed juniper berries to a small pan along with the gin and milk and bring to boil. Bubble for a few minutes, while occasionally stirring.

3. Remove the pan from the heat and season. Set to one side.

4. Remove the outer leaves from the cabbage, and slice into 1/8's. Remove and discard the hard core from each wedge before slicing crossway into strips the width of a child's ruler.

5. Lengthways, halve the leeks and cut into ½" chunks.

6. Add the veggies to a colander and rinse under cold running water.

7. Add the butter to a large saucepan and add the veggies along with any residual water.

8. Sprinkle the bouillon powder over the veggies and season. Cover the pan with a lid and set over moderate heat.

9. Cook for 6 minutes, with the lid in place. Remove the lid every 2 minutes, to toss the cabbage.

10. Take the lid off and cook and toss the cabbage for an additional 5 minutes.

11. Transfer to a colander and thoroughly drain.

12. Return to the pan and keep warm.

13. Place the smaller over low heat, whisk in the fromage frais and season with pepper.

14. Warm the sauce gently while taking care not to boil.

15. Pour the sauce over the cabbage and toss to coat evenly.

16. Enjoy.

vvvvvvvvvvvvvvvvvvvvvvvvvvvvvvvvvvvvvvvvvvvvvvvvvvvvvvvvv

Grilled Cabbage Wedges with Spicy Lime Dressing

Crispy chargrilled cabbage ticks all the boxes, for both taste and texture.

Servings: 8

Total Prep Time: 35mins

Ingredients:

- ¼ cup fresh lime juice
- 1 tsp fish sauce
- ¼ cup extra virgin olive oil
- ¼ cup fresh cilantro leaves
- 2 garlic cloves (peeled, coarsely chopped)
- ½ tsp cayenne pepper
- ½ tsp salt

- ¼ tsp sugar
- 1 head green cabbage
- Canola oil
- Wedges of lime (to serve)

Directions:

1. Heat a grill.

2. In a blender, process the lime juice with the fish sauce, oil, cilantro, garlic, cayenne, salt and sugar, until pale and pulverized. Put to one side.

3. Remove the loosest and toughest outer leaves from the cabbage and cut into 8 equal sized wedges. Do not remove the inner core or stalk.

4. Lightly brush the wedge with canola oil.

5. Arrange the wedges on the grill and cover.

6. Cook until edges of the cabbage are blacked and the cabbage is starting to soften, this will take between 5-7 minutes.

7. Flip each of the wedges over, cover the grill and cook for an additional 5-7 minutes, on the other side.

8. Remove the cabbage from the grill when it is starting to wilt, but remains firm in the center. You may need to reduce the heat to avoid the wedges burning.

9. Remove the cabbage from the grill and arrange on a platter.

10. Pour the dressing over the cabbage and serve with wedges of lime.

vvvvvvvvvvvvvvvvvvvvvvvvvvvvvvvvvvvvvvvvvvvvvvvvvvvvvvvv

Gujarati Cabbage with Potato and Coconut

A traditional Indian dish, Gujarati cabbage made with potato and freshly toasted coconut is fragrant, nutritious, and delicious! What's more, not only does it make a hearty side dish, it would also make a great vegetarian main meal when served with rice.

Servings: 4

Total Prep Time: 30mins

Ingredients:

- 17½ ounces new potatoes (unpeeled, halved)
- 2 tbsp sunflower oil
- Pinch garlic powder

- Pinch onion powder
- 1 tsp black mustard seeds
- 1 tsp cumin seeds
- 2 dry red chilies
- 1 fresh green chili (seeded, sliced thinly)
- 1 sweetheart cabbage (shredded finely)
- Salt
- 2 tbsp fresh coconut (shaved, toasted)
- Juice of ½ a lemon
- Bunch fresh cilantro (chopped roughly)

Directions:

1. In a deep pot of boiling salted water, cook the potatoes for 10 minutes. Drain away the water leaving the potatoes in the pot.

2. Gently crush the potatoes using a fork.

3. In a sauté pan over moderate heat, warm the oil. Add the garlic powder, onion powder, mustard seeds, cumin seeds, and the dried chili. Cook for 3 minutes while stirring before adding the green chili, the cabbage, and a pinch of salt. Sauté for another few minutes.

4. Add the cooked potatoes to the pan and cook for another couple of minutes until the cabbage is bite-tender.

5. Stir in the toasted coconut, lemon juice, and fresh cilantro.

6. Serve straight away.

vvvvvvvvvvvvvvvvvvvvvvvvvvvvvvvvvvvvvvvvvvvvvvvvvvvvvvvvvvv

Irish Colcannon

Colcannon has been Ireland's comfort food of choice since the mid 18th century. With soft buttery cabbage and fluffy potato, it's no wonder this side dish has been a favorite for so many generations. Serve alongside a corned beef dinner for an authentic taste of Ireland.

Servings: 4-6

Total Prep Time: 20mins

Ingredients:

- 1 yellow onion (peeled, diced)
- 3 cups green cabbage (shredded finely)
- ¼ cup water
- 6 cooked potatoes (mashed)
- ¼ cup salted butter
- ¼ cup whole milk
- Salt and black pepper

Directions:

1. To a saucepan over moderately high heat, add the onion, cabbage, and water. Bring to a boil, turn down the heat, cover, and simmer for approximately 8 minutes.

2. Stir in the mashed potato, butter, and milk. Mix well and cook until hot through.

3. Season to taste with salt and black pepper.

4. Serve straight away!

vvvvvvvvvvvvvvvvvvvvvvvvvvvvvvvvvvvvvvvvvvvvvvvvvvvv

Mulled Red Cabbage with Mandarin Oranges

Add a hint of festive flavor to this red cabbage side dish – but don't relegate it to the holidays, it's delicious served all-year round.

Servings: 6-8

Total Prep Time: 1hour 15mins

Ingredients:

- 1 whole mandarin orange
- 15 cloves
- 1½ pounds red cabbage (finely shredded)

- Freshly squeezed zest and juice from 3 mandarin oranges
- 2 red onions (peeled, chopped)
- ¾ cup red wine vinegar
- 5 ounces brown sugar
- 1 tsp mixed spice

Directions:

1. First stud the whole mandarin orange with the cloves and pet to one side.

2. In a large pan, combine the remaining ingredients (red cabbage, mandarin orange zest and juice, onions, red wine vinegar, brown sugar, and mixed spice). Cover with a lid and cook for half an hour.

3. Add the studded mandarin orange, cover and cook for an additional half an hour, until the cabbage is fork tender.

4. Season and enjoy.

vvvvvvvvvvvvvvvvvvvvvvvvvvvvvvvvvvvvvvvvvvvvvvvvvvv

Pointed Cabbage in White Wine with Fennel Seeds

This acidity of this classic cabbage side is the perfect pairing with roast pork.

Servings:6

Total Prep Time: 20mins

Ingredients:

- 2 tbsp olive oil
- 1 tsp fennel seeds
- 1 large onion (peeled, sliced)
- 1 large pointed cabbage (cored, shredded)
- 1 cup dry white wine

- 1 tbsp white wine vinegar
- ½ small bunch coriander (coarsely chopped)

Directions:

1. Ina pan, heat the oil.

2. Add the fennel seeds to the pan and toast for 60 seconds.

3. Stir in the onion and gently cook for a couple of minutes before stirring in the cabbage to evenly coat in olive oil and fennel.

4. Pour in the wine along with the vinegar and reduce by half, this will take 4-5 minutes.

5. On the stove top, simmer for an additional 5 minutes, until the cabbages is sufficiently cooked through the sauce thickened.

6. Fold in the chopped coriander and serve.

vvvvvvvvvvvvvvvvvvvvvvvvvvvvvvvvvvvvvvvvvvvvvvvvvvvvvvvv

Roasted Cabbage Coleslaw with Hazelnuts and Honey Lemon Dressing

Crispy cabbage, crunchy toasted hazelnuts and a sweet yet tart dressing is the best-ever side salad.

Servings: 4-6

Total Prep Time: 30mins

Ingredients:

- ½ head red cabbage
- ½ head Savoy cabbage
- Olive oil

- 1¼ cups hazelnuts

Dressing:

- Olive oil
- 3 tbsp freshly squeezed lemon juice
- 1 tsp honey
- Flaky sea salt and black pepper
- 1 ounce Gruyere cheese (to garnish)

Directions:

1. Heat the broiler.

2. Core the red and Savoy cabbage and roughly shred.

3. Place the shredded cabbage in a bowl and lightly toss with olive oil.

4. In a single layer spread the shredded cabbage out onto a large baking sheet.

5. Broil the cabbage until the shreds are starting to char, this will take between 5-7 minutes.

6. Stir the cabbage and broil for an additional 5 minutes. The cabbage is sufficiently cooked when it is crisp on the edges rather than cooked through.

7. Remove the cabbage from the broiler and put to one side to cool for 2-3 minutes.

8. Turn the broiler off and preheat the main oven to 350 degrees F.

9. Chop the hazelnuts and spread them out on a baking sheet, bake in the oven until lightly toasted for 5-10 minutes.

10. In a bowl for the dressing, whisk the 1 tablespoon of olive oil, the lemon juice, and honey.

11. Toss the cabbage with the dressing and season to taste. Toss with 1 cup of toasted hazelnuts.

12. Spread on a large serving platter and garnish with the remaining nuts.

13. Scatter with Gruyere cheese and serve.

vvvvvvvvvvvvvvvvvvvvvvvvvvvvvvvvvvvvvvvvvvvvvvvvvvvvvvvvvvvvvv

Sautéed Cabbage with Spicy Mustard

Cabbage gets a makeover with hot mustard and spicy horseradish.

Servings: 4

Total Prep Time: 30mins

Ingredients:

- 3 tbsp unsalted butter
- 1 large onion (peeled, halved lengthways, thinly sliced)
- 2 ½ pounds green cabbage (quartered, cored, cut crosswise into ¼ "thick strips)
- ¾ tsp salt
- 1 cup water
- 1 tbsp coarse grain mustard
- 1 tsp prepared horseradish
- 1 tsp all-purpose flour

Directions:

1. Over medium-high heat, in a heavy frying pan, heat the butter until the foam subsides.

2. Add the onion to the pan and while occasionally stirring cook for 5 minutes, until gently browned.

3. Stir the cabbage, salt and ½ cup of water and while covered, cook while occasionally stirring for 10-12 minutes, or until the cabbage is just tender.

4. Transfer the cabbage to a platter.

5. In a frying pan, whisk the mustard together with the horseradish and flour.

6. Add the remaining water and whisk until thoroughly combined.

7. Simmer for a couple of minutes, before stirring into the cabbage.

8. Season.

vvvvvvvvvvvvvvvvvvvvvvvvvvvvvvvvvvvvvvvvvvvvvvvvvvvvvv

Warm Pecan-Cabbage Slaw

This warm slaw with crunchy pecans and a buttery mustard drizzle is a more filling and satisfying side for your favorite cookout dishes.

Servings: 6

Total Prep Time: 15mins

Ingredients:

- ½ cup grated carrot
- 4 cups shredded cabbage
- ¼ cup green onions (thinly sliced)
- ½ tsp kosher salt
- 2 tbsp water
- ¼ tsp black pepper

- 1 tsp Dijon mustard
- 1 tbsp melted butter
- ¼ cup toasted pecans (chopped)

Directions:

1. Add the carrot, cabbage, green onions, salt, water, and black pepper to a saucepan over moderate heat and cook, covered, for several minutes. Drain away any excess water.

2. Transfer the mixture to a serving bowl.

3. Stir together the mustard and melted butter. Drizzle the mixture over the vegetables.

4. Sprinkle over the chopped pecans and serve.

vvvvvvvvvvvvvvvvvvvvvvvvvvvvvvvvvvvvvvvvvvvvvvvvvvv

Made in the USA
Monee, IL
12 April 2025

15602126R00066